A is for Alligator

A is for Alligator

Draw and Tell Tales from A–Z

Dianne de Las Casas and Marita Gentry

 **LIBRARIES UNLIMITED**

AN IMPRINT OF ABC-CLIO, LLC
Santa Barbara, California • Denver, Colorado • Oxford, England

Library of Congress Cataloging-in-Publication Data

de las Casas, Dianne
    A is for alligator : draw and tell tales from A-Z / Dianne de Las
  Casas and Marita Gentry.
      p. cm.
   ISBN 978-1-59884-929-5 (pbk : alk. paper) -- ISBN 978-1-59884-930-1
(ebook) 1. Drawing--Study and teaching. 2. Storytelling--United
States. 3. Activity programs in education--United States. 4.
Storytelling in education. I. Title.
  LC1592.D45 2011
  372.67'7--dc22   2011010416

ISBN: 978-1-59884-929-5
EISBN: 978-1-59884-930-1

15 14 13 12 11   1 2 3 4 5

This book is also available on the World Wide Web as an eBook.
Visit www.abc-clio.com for details.

Libraries Unlimited
An Imprint of ABC-CLIO, LLC

ABC-CLIO, LLC
130 Cremona Drive, P.O. Box 1911
Santa Barbara, California 93116-1911

This book is printed on acid-free paper ∞
Manufactured in the United States of America

For Marita

You are a joy to work with.
A is for Awesome Artist!

—Dianne de Las Casas

For my students . . .

Both past and present.
I draw inspiration from you.

—Marita Gentry

CONTENTS

INTRODUCTION

I love exploring new ways to tell stories. In *Handmade Tales: Stories to Make and Take*, there are two draw and tell tales in the book. When I perform a draw and tell story, I really enjoy watching the audience's delight when the lines translate into a picture. It's even more impressive when the lines of the picture have lines from a story to accompany it. Together, both kinds of "lines" draw meaning.

Marita Gentry and I have created several children's books together (*The Cajun Cornbread Boy, Madame Poulet and Monsieur Roach, The Gigantic Sweet Potato, There's a Dragon in the Library*, and *Dinosaur Mardi Gras*). When we promote our books, we perform together. I tell the story as she illustrates live. I am always amazed at how quickly Marita can render a drawing, as is the audience. Seeing Marita in action gave me the idea for this collaboration. While I can do simple draw and tell tales, I needed a talented partner to create drawings in this book.

We worked "backwards." Usually, I write the story, and Marita illustrates it. This time, she drew the pictures first, and then I wrote the accompanying stories. We worked together to select animals to represent each letter. The result is fantastic, and I know students will love being able to draw and tell a story at the same time.

Marita and I both work extensively in schools, doing teaching artist residencies in the classroom. Kids love drawing these simple animals. When the lines are broken down step by step, it's so much easier to create a picture. It's a "Eureka!" moment for a child when the illustration is completed. Coupled with the story, the drawing and the tale work together to help a student with recall, sequencing, and retelling strategies. These stories are also great for librarians, teachers, child caregivers, camp counselors, and parents. As long as you have a writing implement and a piece of paper, you can keep a child thoroughly entertained!

Marita and I hope you enjoy drawing and telling these tales as much as we enjoyed creating them. Here's to draw and tell fun. Happy Tales to You!

Warmly,
Dianne de Las Casas
dianne@storyconnection.net
www.storyconnection.net

If you are going to use these draw and tell tales with elementary-age students, it is best to draw and tell the story yourself first, before you begin illustration instruction. If you are working with Grades 6 and above, they can usually follow along as you draw and tell the story. Tell the story at a steady pace. This will allow you to coordinate the simultaneous telling and drawing. Any necessary actions in the story are noted in the text.

When working with students and instructing them on how to draw, encourage them to relax both their body and their grip on the pencil. It is difficult to draw when you are clenching your pencil. When drawing, it is hard to make a fatal error. Most mistakes can be easily corrected, usually without erasing. Erasing is not bad, but a student that constantly erases shows a tendency for perfection. Let the students know that most mistakes can be corrected with a little imagination.

The size and placement of the letter is important. Is the letter small? Is it large? How big is the finished drawing in relation to the letter? Instruct the students accordingly. In "A is for Alligator," for example, the "A" would be drawn on a vertical piece of paper taking up about one third of the bottom of the paper. Once the students create the "A," have them turn the paper so that it is horizontal. If everything is in order and the letter looks right, then drawing the rest of the picture can begin.

As you draw the picture, be sure that the students are keeping pace with you. If they fall behind, slow down and give a few directional instructions. For example, "This line should be straight and close to the left edge of the paper. It touches the end of the curved line at the top of the paper." Specific directions aid in the drawing and enhances a student's skills with spatial relationships. Use words such as "top," "bottom," and "middle."

Drawing a subject step-by-step enhances creative thinking. It gives the students a success story and a jumping-off point. For example, the alligator would be drawn together in class. After the students achieve success with the drawing, the students can then be instructed to take their skills a step further by drawing a background to illustrate the story. This draws on their prior knowledge and allows them to use contextual clues to create a new drawing. Varying results are good. No two students will draw the same way. It demonstrates creative thinking and originality.

Another way to encourage creativity is to perform the draw and tell in class and then introduce the animal in another lesson. Allow the students to draw the animal from memory. For example, you can say, "Remember the alligator we drew with a story last week? This week we are studying swamp animals and I want you to draw an alligator in the swamp. This time, you will draw the alligator by yourself." Be sure to have a visual aid ready, such as a picture of the alligator from the previous week. Inspired by the visual cue, they will draw from their memories, usually rendering a much more elaborate drawing.

Once students master the drawing, encourage them to practice drawing and telling the tale at the same time. Learning the story will help them remember the drawing and vice versa. The telling of the tale will aid in their sequencing skills, their recall and retelling abilities, and their comprehension of the story.

Draw and tell tales allow students to go on an imagination journey. It allows them to experience the familiar yet explore new horizons. The drawings and the tales work together to allow students to draw their own success stories.

 is for *Alligator*

A is for ALEX and ANDY.

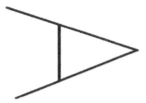

The two boys sat by their house, bored. "Let's find something to do," said one boy to the other.

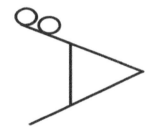

So they began walking. They walked over a big hill.

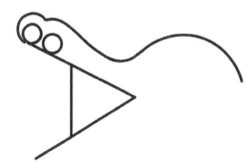

They walked over a little hill.

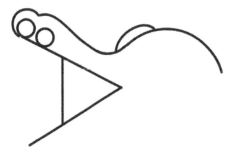

Suddenly, Alex found something on the ground. It was a hook!

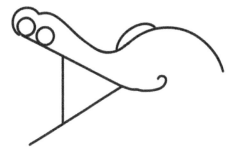

Andy found a piece of string. Together, they shouted, "Let's go fishing!"

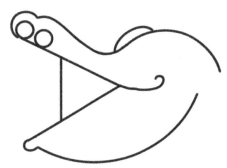

So they walked to the river.

They found a stick and made a fishing pole.

They sat down on top of a rock and began to fish.

Alex felt something tugging on the line, so he pulled hard on the pole with his hands.

When he pulled on the fishing pole, all he could see was a giant eye!

Following the eye was a mouth full of GIGANTIC sharp . . . TEETH!
[*Pause and allow the children to chime in the answer.*]

Alex and Andy caught an . . . ALLIGATOR! [*Pause and allow the children to chime in the answer.*]

They ran home as quickly as they could and NEVER complained about being bored again!

 is for *Bear*

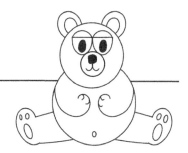

B is for BILLY, and Billy saw a big animal in the forest.

The animal had wide eyes. Billy asked, "Why do you have such big eyes?

The animal answered, "The better to see you with, my friend."

The animal had a hefty sniffer. Billy asked, "Why do you have such a big nose?"

The animal answered, "The better to smell you with, my friend."

The animal had a giant furry head. Billy asked, "Why do you have such a big head?"

The animal answered, "The better to think with, my friend."

The animal had large ears. Billy asked, "Why do you have such big ears?"

The animal said, "The better to hear you with, my friend."

The animal had a gigantic tummy. Billy asked, "Why do you have such a big belly?"

The animal answered, "The better to eat more, my friend."

The animal had thick legs. Billy asked, "Why do you have such big legs?"

The animal answered, "The better to chase with, my friend."

The animal had enormous arms. Billy asked, shivering, "W-w-why do you have such big arms?!"

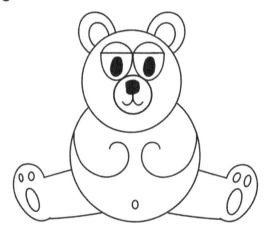

The animal answered, "The better to . . . [*Pause dramatically.*] hug you with, my friend!" The animal gave Billy a BIG BEAR HUG! [*Hug someone in the audience.*]

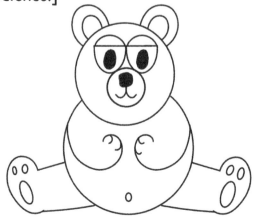

 is for *Cat*

C is for CORNER. Mortimer was deathly afraid to come out of his corner.

Something was out there, and it was big! If he ran this way, maybe he would go unnoticed.

If he ran that way, maybe he could sneak by the CREEPY CREATURE.

So Mortimer tiptoed across the floor with his little feet.

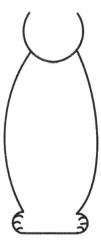

Mortimer zipped through the house.

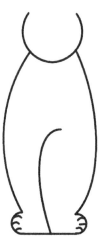

He quickly scooted into a small hole.

Mortimer peeked out of his hiding place.

Mortimer saw its hind legs.

Its tail was whipping back and forth, just waiting.

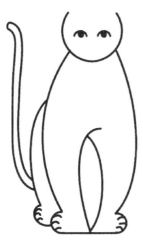

Mortimer was deathly afraid of this CRUEL ... CAT!

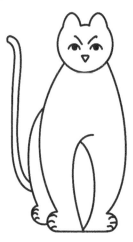

Fortunately, Mortimer was a clever mouse. The hole he was in was a doggie door, and CLYDE THE CAT was afraid of Pounder the Pit Bull! C is for scaredy ... CAT!

So Mortimer escaped, and CLYDE had to sharpen his claws for another day!

 **is for *Dog***

D is for DOTTIE. She wanted someone to cuddle.

WHERE should Dottie go? She walked out the door.

She traveled AROUND the neighborhood.

First, she went to her friend, Debby's house, but no one was home.

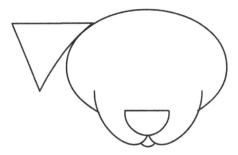

Then she went to her friend Daisy's house, but again, no one was home.

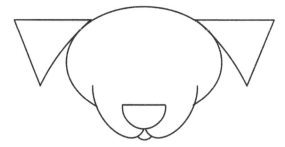

She looked down and saw something.

It started running around and around her, making her DIZZY.

Dottie found a DALMATIAN DOG.

The DOG was covered with DOTS so Dottie named her Spottie.

Dottie brought Spottie home and had someone to cuddle.

 is for **Elephant**

E is for Ellie. Ellie's *greatest* dream was to join the circus!

She began walking toward the city.

She discovered a playground in the middle of a *large* park.

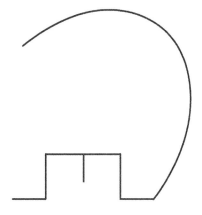

Ellie slid down the slide—WEEEE! But the slide broke.

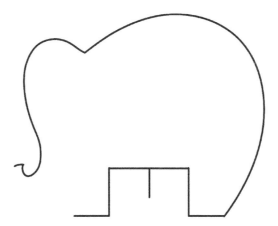

So she followed the path up through the park and down the sidewalk.

That's when Ellie saw a *gigantic* tent.

Ellie looked inside. It was the perfect place for her!

She hid behind two barrels.

She saw the ringmaster with his whip.

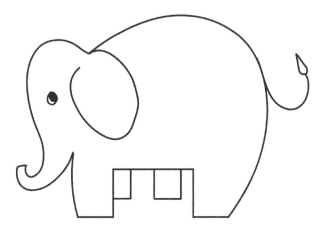

But Ellie couldn't hide for long. All eyes were on her. She drew ENORMOUS attention.

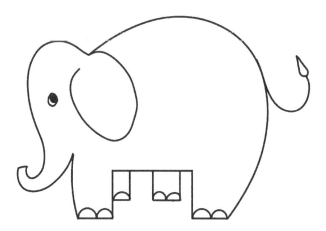

Everyone couldn't help but notice Ellie. She was the most spectacular ELEPHANT they had ever seen. Ellie joined the circus and made it BIG! E is for ELLIE the EXTRAORDINARY ELEPHANT! [*Embellish Ellie as you wish.*]

 is for *Frog*

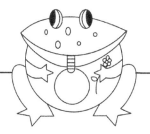

F is for FIVE aliens. They were heading to Earth to collect FLOWER specimens.

F

They sat in their chairs and prepared for their long journey.

They craft flew faster than a speeding bullet.

When they landed, the ladder descended from the ship.

The ship hovered over the ground.

The aliens looked out of their window.

As their space ship hovered above the ground, they couldn't believe what they saw!

They had landed near a large pond.

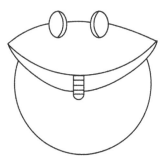

They left the ship and began collecting specimens, gathering as many flowers as their hands could hold.

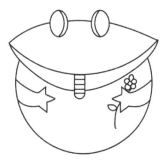

That's when they came across a FOREIGN FIGURE, unlike any creature they had ever seen before! They circled around it.

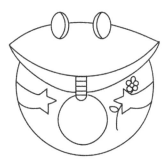

It had legs that leaped and funny feet!

The big green monster stared right at them and stuck its tongue out, slurping. The FIVE aliens ran for their lives. They boarded their spaceship and flew away. F is for FEARSOME FROG!

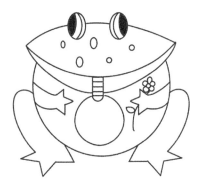

 is for *Giraffe*

G is for GINA. Gina loved GARDENS.

Gina walked to her garden.

Her garden was in the GREENHOUSE.

From her greenhouse ceiling hung baskets of buds.

Gina planted seeds.

She watered the seeds.

Then she walked up the stone path to check on her other flowers.

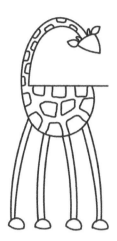

She loved what she saw!

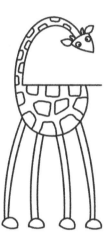

A flower had GROWN. Gina's garden was GORGEOUS! G is for GINA, the GARDENING GIRAFFE.

 is for *Horse*

H is for HANNAH.

Hannah loved baking. Her favorite fruit was blueberries.

Hannah decided to make blueberry muffins.

She adjusted the knobs on the oven so that it could warm up.

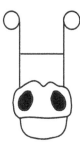

She opened the curtains to let light into the kitchen.

Then she began baking. She measured her ingredients with scoops.

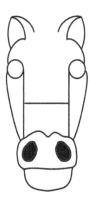

When the muffins were done, she topped them with whipped cream.

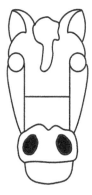

That's when Hannah noticed the eyes staring at her through the window!

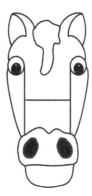

It was her horse, Heidi. Those blueberry muffins sure smelled good!

So Hannah shared her blueberry muffins with Heidi. H is for HUNGRY HORSE!

 is for Iguana

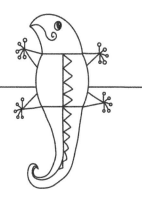

I is for Isabella. Isabella lived in the Land of the Shining Sun. More than anything, she longed for a friend.

One day, Isabella was sitting by her window.

She heard the wind whispering from the sea.

She loved her little house by the ocean.

From her window, she could see the waves crest and pound against the shore. Everything was perfect except that she was lonely.

One day, under the warm, shining sun, she had a visitor.

It was a lizard. The lizard spoke and said, "I am INDIGO and I have traveled a long way to be here. I traveled over tall mountains."

The lizard said, "I traveled through tree-filled jungles."

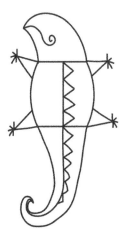

The lizard said, "In fact, I have been traveling for many moons, looking for a friend."

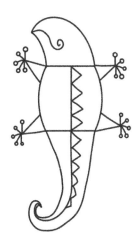

Isabella was happy. She finally found a friend. Together, Isabella and Indigo listened to the wind, watched the waves, and basked in the warm sun of the land of Mexico. I is for INCREDIBLE IGUANA.

 is for *Jackrabbit*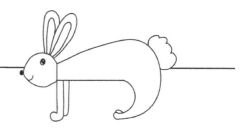

J is for JUMPIN' JELLYBEANS!

Who is that critter sneaking around the garden?

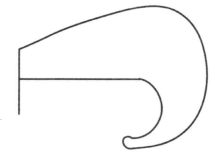

He likes to creep behind things.

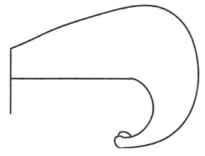

He likes to hide the shovel!

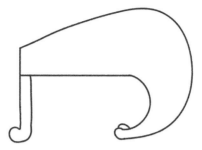

It's because he's trying to avoid Mr. Farmer and his watchful eye.

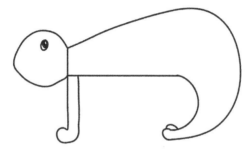

That little critter loves to eat all the cabbage.

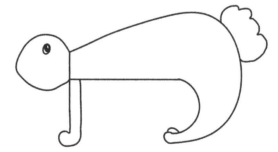

That little critter loves to eat all the carrots, big and small!

He sniffs out all the best veggies for himself! He munches, crunches, and lunches with a smile on his face.

Better watch out because he can leap faster than the wind can blow! J is for JUMPING JACKRABBIT!

 is for *Kangaroo*

K is for Kelly, who lived in the dry Outback.

R is for Rain. Kelly wished that rain would fall!

She really wanted to see a pond fill up with water.

It would be a grand pool with a slide!

There would be a diving board to jump from.

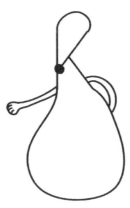

There would be a deep end and a shallow end for all the kids.

Kelly looked up. There was not a cloud in the sky.

So Kelly put away her flippers.

She began hopping away.

Suddenly, Joey poked his head out of the pouch and asked, "Mommy, when are we going swimming?" K is for KOOKY KANGAROO.

 is for **Lion**

L is for LOUIE.

L

Louie had a metal nail and an idea!

So Louie ran out into the middle of the field. It was raining.

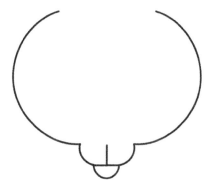

Louie's head lit up like a lightbulb when he had an idea!

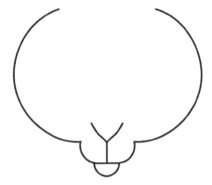

He could smell the electricity in the air.

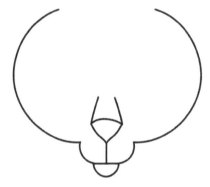

Louie looked up into the night sky.

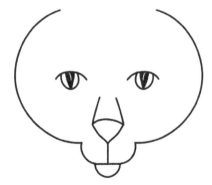

Louie heard thunder!

Then suddenly lightning flashed!

Louie dropped the metal nail, but it was too late. Louie was struck, and his hair stood straight up! It hit the nail on the head. L is for LOUIE the LIGHTNING LION.

 **is for _Monkey_**

M is for Mary.

Mary wanted an ice cream cone.

Mary wanted two flavors and two cherries on top!

So she walked around the neighborhood, looking for the ice cream truck.

She thought she heard the truck near the pond, but it wasn't there. All she found was a little girl's bow.

She thought she heard the truck by some trees, but it wasn't there either.

She walked a little further to the lake.

That's when she saw something swinging from the trees!

It had small ears and a long tail. It looked straight at her!

There was a puddle of ice cream on the ground. It had stolen all the ice cream cones and eaten them! M is for MISCHIEVOUS MONKEY!

 **is for _Nightingale_**

N is for NANCY.

Z

W is for Warbler.

⅗

Nancy was a warbler. She loved to sing. Any time she opened her mouth, melodious notes appeared.

↗

Besides singing, she adored flying through the clouds.

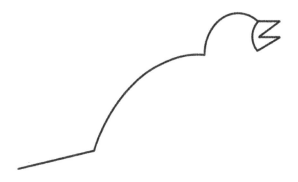

She was top-notch at swooping.

She was excellent at fast curves and zooming zips.

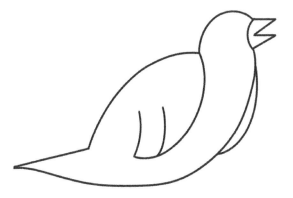

And Nancy always landed on her feet. N is for NANCY the NOTEWORTHY NIGHTINGALE!

 is for **Owl**

O is for Oh my goodness! Look at this egg!

This egg hatched one bird who has the smarts of two eggs!

This bird watches over all the other birds while they are sleeping.

He is considered the "professor" of the woods because he is so wise.

If you ask him a question, he'll never look down his beak at you.

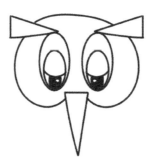

He is a rotund fellow.

The animals of the forest look to him as a "judge." He should wear a robe or a cape!

When you are in troubled waters, you can be sure that Professor O will have a sage answer.

O is for OBSERVANT OWL.

 **P** is for *Penguin*

P is for PERCY.

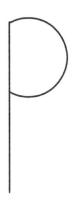

Percy was getting ready for a PARTY so he had to put on his best. Percy put on a bow tie.

He put on his best suit.

He spiked his hair.

He donned his "dancing shoes."

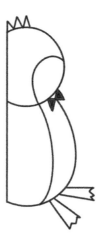

He looked in the mirror and said, "You're lookin' PERFECT!"

Percy walked in the direction of the celebration with his fancy flippers.

Then Percy got down. [*Move penguin around as if he is dancing.*] He did the bop, the hop, the skip, and the boogie. He danced the foxtrot, the tango, and the hokey-pokey. P is for PERCY the PEPPY PARTY PENGUIN!

 is for **Quail**

Q is for QUEEN.

The queen wanted dinner and QUICKLY. So the cook grabbed his pan and knife.

He went on a QUEST and walked in the direction of the forest.

He came to a large lake. He walked around the edge of the lake.

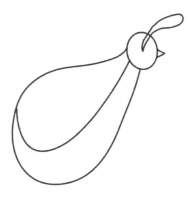

He searched all the bushes, even the ones covered with thorns.

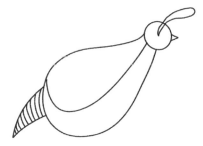

The cook heard something and ran toward it.

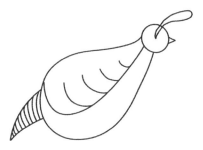

The cook saw that it was a bird with a spotted belly and a big QUILL.

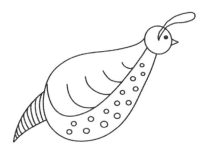

The bird was the perfect poultry for the queen's pesto! But the bird was QUIVERING and QUAKING, so the cook set it free. Q is for QUAIL.

R is for *Rooster*

R is for RISE and shine! It's morning time!

Rhett opened his eyes. It was time for REHEARSAL!

If he was going to be a star, he had to be like eggs and get crackin'! So Rhett got dressed. He combed and waddled to the barn.

Rhett grabbed his spoon and began to croon.

All the barn animals woke up. It was like a lightning storm!

Bessie Cow asked, "What's all the RACKET, Rhett? You cracked one of Henny's eggs!"

Rhett laughed. "I'm sorry. I was singing my favorite song, 'Somewhere Over the Rainbow.' I'm rehearsing for the big time."

The ducks quacked up. Ducky Lucky said, "Rhett, with that voice, I think you ought to stick to something less ROWDY." Rhett said, "You know what? You're right. With these loosey-goosey legs, I should be a dancer!"

The next morning, all the animals awoke again to a ROUSING RACKET. Turkey Lurkey cried out, "What in tarnation is that?" Rhett answered, "I'm rehearsing for the big time. I'm tap dancing!!" The barn animals went shopping for . . . earplugs. R is for RHETT the ROCKIN' ROOSTER.

 **S** is for *Shark*

S is for SANDY.

Sandy went fishing and baited her hook.

SOMETHING began tugging on her line. Sandy looked down and saw that it had beady eyes and sharp teeth!

Sandy STRUGGLED. She pulled her line in but the fish fought against her.

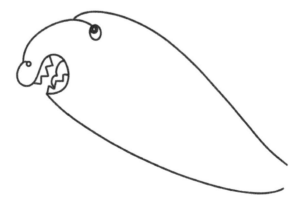

It felt like an anchor weighing her down.

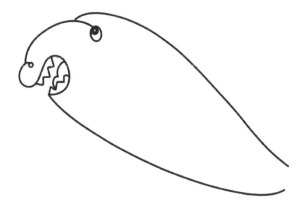

Then Sandy saw what she was afraid of . . . it had a dorsal fin! Sandy screamed!

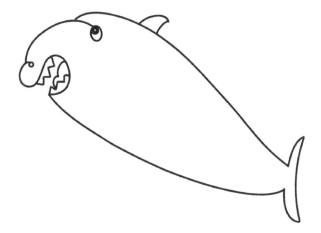

S is for SUPER SCARY . . . SHARK!

 T is for *Turtle*

T is for TINA.

Tina had a TINY umbrella.

It was raining so hard that she was getting wet. She needed something warm and dry.

So she tried on a hat. But she was still getting wet.

Then she tried on a helmet. She was still getting wet.

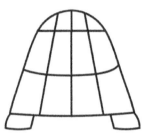

Then Tina heard a loud CRACK in the sky. It was THUNDER. So Tina went home and TUCKED herself in.

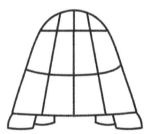

In the morning, the storm was gone. Tina came out.

She looked around and smiled. TODAY was TERRIFIC!

T is for TINA the TINY TURTLE.

 is for *Unicorn*

Once UPON a time . . .

There was a pauper whose greatest possessions were two gold coins.

More than anything, he wanted to find a magical treasure. So he went on a quest. He searched inside a deep cave.

Inside the cave he found a princess' hat!

He searched inside another cave.

There he found a beauty with long curly locks.

She had pretty eyes and a sweet smile.

The pauper had found one of the kingdom's greatest treasures indeed! U is for Unbelievable Unicorn!

V is for *Vulture*

V is for VICTOR.

Victor went on a camping trip and set up a tent. Then he had to find something to eat.

So he traveled down the river.

He searched in an area filled with lots of bushes.

That's when he saw an egg!

Just as Victor was about to grab the egg, it cracked in half.

Out came a funny-looking bird. Victor stared at the bird and saw what it was. V is for VULTURE.

 **is for Whale**

W is for WILLIE.

One day, Willie decided to go on a fishing trip. He boarded his little boat, the *Mariner,* and cast his line.

It didn't go far enough, so Willie had to pull it back in and cast his line again. This time it was a long line.

WAVES began rocking the little boat. Willie caught something big!

It was WRIGGLING and WIGGLING on his line. Willie couldn't believe his eyes!

When Willie realized what he caught, he let go of the line. W is for WONDERFUL WHALE.

The WHALE waved goodbye to Willie and thanked him with a spray of WATER. Willie couldn't wait to get home and share his adventure. It was a WHALE of a tale!

 **is for _X-Ray Fish_**

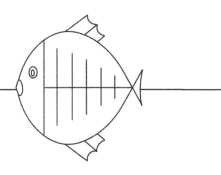

X marks the spot.

It was going to be an eXcellent adventure for XAVIER. He was going to a fishing tournament! He raced out of the house.

Xavier ran to the marina.

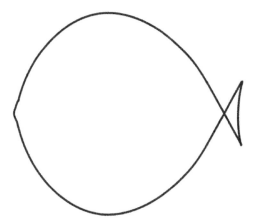

Xavier looked around and opened his mouth to call for his friend.

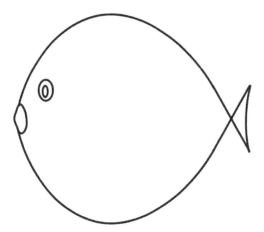

T is for TOMMY who snuck up on Xavier. "Boo!"

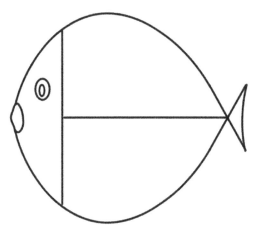

Xavier and Tommy walked to the end of the pier to see the tournament.

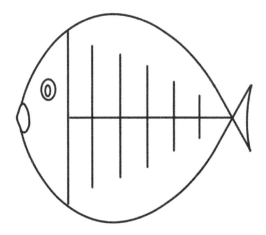

They saw all the fishermen casting their lines from the end of the pier.

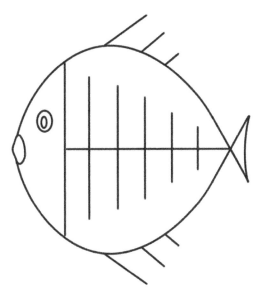

One of the fishermen caught something eXciting. When Xavier eXamined the man's catch, he couldn't believe his eyes! X is for eXtraordinary X-RAY FISH!

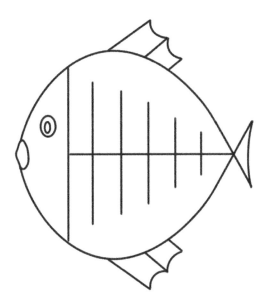

 is for *Yak*

Y is for YANCY.

Yancy was growing a YELLOW flower.

The flower sprouted from a little bowl.

The bowl was inside a terrarium.

One day, as Yancy was looking at his little bud, he noticed something.

He YEARNED for a snack. He walked outside, into the YARD, and onto the grass.

His neighbor was baking and he could smell it. That made Yancy crave a YUMMY muffin.

So Yancy chopped up some nuts.

Then he cut up some bananas. He mixed the batter and baked. Y is for YANCY the YOUTHFUL YAK who made YUMMY banana nut muffins.

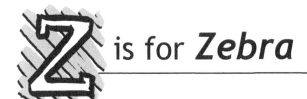 is for *Zebra*

Z is for Zack.

Zack loved running around the racetrack.

He knew that he was different. The other runners looked down upon him, but he didn't care.

He loved running from point A to point B and feeling the wind in his hair.

Zack looked at the other racers.

Even though he didn't look or act like them, he knew that he could run circles around his competition.

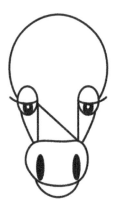

It was time for the big race. Everyone lined up. Zack opened his ears and listened carefully. "BOOM!" the gun went off. It was time to race!

Zack ran down the straight-away and crossed the finish line first. Zack won the race!

From that time on, Zack was called "Racing Stripes." Z is for ZACK the ZIPPY ZEBRA!

ABOUT THE AUTHORS

DIANNE DE LAS CASAS is a celebrated author, award-winning storyteller, and recording artist. Her work has earned rave reviews in *School Library Journal, Booklist,* and *Kirkus.* She performs at schools, libraries, festivals, and special events and is a frequent speaker at national and state library and education conferences. Dianne's professional books include *Tales from the 7,000 Isles: Filipino Folk Stories, Tell Along Tales: Playing with Participation Stories, Stories on Board: Creating Board Games from Favorite Tales, Scared Silly: 25 Tales to Tickle and Thrill, The Story Biz Handbook, Tangram Tales: Story Theater Using the Ancient Chinese Puzzle, Handmade Tales: Stories to Make and Take, Kamishibai Story Theater: The Art of Picture Telling,* and *Story Fest: Creating Story Theater Scripts.* Her children's books include *The Cajun Cornbread Boy, Madame Poulet and Monsieur Roach, Mama's Bayou, The Gigantic Sweet Potato, There's a Dragon in the Library, The House That Witchy Built,* and *Blue Frog: The Legend of Chocolate.* Visit her website at www. storyconnection.net.

MARITA GENTRY is a professional artist and has her own painting and teaching studio, Studio Marita, in southern Louisiana. Her vivid illustrations have earned her numerous awards and commissions. An accomplished teacher, she is involved in several artist-in-residence programs each year, helping schools enliven their walls with magnificent murals. Marita has collaborated with Dianne de Las Casas, illustrating many of her children's books including *The Cajun Cornbread Boy, Madame Poulet and Monsieur Roach, The Gigantic Sweet Potato,* and *There's a Dragon in the Library.*

CPSIA information can be obtained at www.ICGtesting.com
Printed in the USA
LVOW02s1432071013

355805LV00016B/551/P